Aslan in Our World

A Companion to *The Lion, the Witch, and the Wardrobe*

By Cate McDermott

The Sibling Writery
SW

Dedicated to my family
With thanks for all their encouragement
And with all my love

Table of Contents

Aslan in Our World: A Companion to The Lion, the Witch, and the Wardrobe

Study Questions for Chapter One

1. How are the four children different? How would you expect that they would each participate individually in the coming adventure? Would you share the Gospel in a different way with Lucy than with Edmund? With Susan? With Peter? Would you expect them to react differently? How should we take into consideration people's individual backgrounds and personalities when we first introduce them to our Christian faith?

2. Re-read the passage on pages 5-6[*], beginning with "Of course it *would* be raining" and ending with "that was how the adventures began." Have you ever found that a commonplace or even disagreeable incident actually turned out to be part of God's plans for you? Discuss.

3. Did you notice that Lucy "thought it would be worth while trying the door of the wardrobe, even though she felt almost sure that it would be locked" (page 6)? Have you ever met people who *wouldn't* have thought it worthwhile to try, who consider it wiser to assume that the pathway to discover the Truth is shut off from us? What are some different ways in which different people might have an opportunity offered to them to discover the Truth? Some

---

[*]Page numbers are from the hardcover 2007 edition by HarperCollins Publishers (the slipcover boxed set)

relevant Scripture references here are John 1:9 and 18:37, and Acts 17:27-31.

4. Think about what Lucy says on page 9: "I can always get back if anything goes wrong." Is she right? When people first begin searching for God—even if they don't realize at first that that is what they are doing—and they find that they are getting into more than they bargained for, can they so easily get out of it again? Look at Luke 14:28, and discuss what Jesus means here by "counting the cost" before becoming His disciple. Then go back and read Luke 9:62. What are the consequences of turning back from one's search for God?

5. Why do you think a quite ordinary wardrobe was the way into the mysterious wood? What other ordinary material things might have connections to realities beyond this physical world? Can you think of any Bible stories that point to this?

Study Questions for Chapter Two

1. What do you think of the name "Daughter of Eve" by which Mr. Tumnus addresses Lucy? What is it that makes humans different from all other creatures? Read Genesis 1:26-31 about the distinguishing identity God gave to all humans, and discuss the ethical and spiritual responsibility this places on us.

2. On page 13, Mr. Tumnus assumes that "eternal summer reigns around the bright city of War Drobe" simply because Lucy had said it was summer *now* where she came from, which she had also not said was a city, but rather "not countries at all . . . just back there" (page 12). What sort of generalizations do people often make about matters (especially of religion or culture) of which they are ignorant?

3. Did you notice the last two titles listed on Mr. Tumnus' bookshelf (page 15)? What ideas in our own culture about what is (or might be) mythical do they remind you of? Do you think that Mr. Tumnus may have doubted the existence of humans before he actually met one? (See page 11, where Mr. Tumnus mentions that he has "never seen a Son of Adam or a Daughter of Eve before.") What kind of experiences do people need to have in order to know whether something is true or mythical—or is experience not necessarily essential to having such knowledge at all?

4. What do you think of Lucy's reaction to Mr. Tumnus' confession, the balance she tried to strike between "be[ing] truthful and yet not be[ing] too hard on him" (page 19)? How would you deal with a situation in which you wanted to be sympathetic, understanding,

and forgiving towards someone you liked who had done something wrong, without letting them think that it was all right for them to have done the wrong in the first place? Try to think of some examples of how the old saying "hate sin and love the sinner" could play out in everyday life and situations.

5. Did you figure out what Mr. Tumnus was up to before Lucy did? What signs might indicate to us that even very nice people that we enjoy being with are involved in wrong activities? Lucy says (on page 19), "I'm sure you wouldn't do anything of the sort," and yet Mr. Tumnus *was*. Can we assume that something is all right just because it hasn't yet shown signs of being wrong, or do we need to be very sure it is right before we get involved in it? Read 2 Corinthians 6:14-18, 1 Thessalonians 5:21-22, and 1 John 4:1.

6. Read what Mr. Tumnus says about "the four thrones at Cair Paravel" on page 20. Does it strike you as odd that he appeals to something that he is not sure "will ever happen at all" as his only means of rescue? How might his doubts have aided in leading him into working for the Witch in the first place?

7. Is there a difference between Mr. Tumnus' being "in the pay of the White Witch" (page 19) just to protect himself, and the spy trees who are "on her side" (page 21)? And if there is a difference, could it arise from the fact that Mr. Tumnus knows the Witch is evil and is angry with himself and repentant for succumbing to the temptation to serve her, while the trees and other spies on her side actually want her evil ways? What is the distinction between doing something wrong (sinning) and actually being an evil, ungodly person?

Study Questions for Chapter Three

1. Why do you think that even Lucy could not see Narnia in the wardrobe when she came back with the others? Has it ever happened to you (I know it has to me) that truths and realities which appear quite obvious at some times become distant and difficult to believe in under other circumstances, especially others' disbelief?

2. Have you ever been in a situation like Lucy, where you knew you were right but had no way of proving it or convincing those who disagreed with you? How might you try to convince people of the existence of things which play no part in their current outlook on life? Read 1 Peter 3:13-17 (especially verse 15), and see if you can find encouragement in these verses for dealing with such situations.

3. Read again what Lucy thinks to herself on page 27: "she was beginning to wonder herself whether Narnia and the Faun had not been a dream." How can constant exposure to those who deny the Truth make it seem less convincing? What causes us to have doubts about things? Is actual experience enough to prevent us from ever doubting the reality of the experience, or is something else necessary to assure us of what is and is not true?

4. Do you think there is a connection between Edmund's careless foolishness in shutting the door of the wardrobe without thinking (page 28) and his unkind nature? Read the Book of Proverbs (if you don't have time to read the whole thing, especially note Proverbs 1:7, 13:10-20, 15:21, 16:16-22, and 27:12), and talk over

the connection, in God's eyes, that there is between foolishness and sinfulness and pride.

5. Read over what Edmund's first reaction to Narnia was, on pages 29-30, and then go back and read what Lucy's was, on pages 8-9. How were they different? What do you think this says about the kind of people Lucy and Edmund are, and how spiritually mature each of them is, respectively?

6. Should Edmund have gone away immediately upon meeting the strange lady, simply because "[h]e did not like the way she looked at him" (page 33)? Do we need concrete proof in order to recognize that something is evil, or is there a way to know this even before something happens to definitely demonstrate whether someone or something can harm us? What abilities does God provide us with so that we can tell the difference between good and evil? For further discussion, read Malachi 3:16-18 and Romans 12:1-2.

Study Questions for Chapter Four

1.   What did you think about the Queen's sudden change of manner towards Edmund? Were you surprised? In your own experience, have you found that people are more likely to try to threaten you or to flatter you into joining them in doing something wrong? In what circumstances, if ever, is it wise to compromise with those who were earlier completely opposed to us? Read Matthew 7:15. Would it have been better for Edmund if he had known and heeded this warning?

2.   Read about Edmund's poor manners on page 37, and then go back to page 12 and notice how polite Lucy was in addressing "Mr. Tumnus." Are manners and other matters of cultured and civilized behavior linked with matters of what is actually right and wrong, or is it simply a question of differing tastes and traditions? Discuss the implications of these contrasting views.

3.   Was Edmund at fault for wanting more Turkish Delight, since he could not help the fact that it magically made him want more, and he hadn't known that to begin with? But he had asked for sweets, which always have the potential to be eaten in unhealthy portions. Do we ever have an excuse to blame God or circumstances or our own ignorance when we fall into sinful or harmful behavior? Some Scriptures dealing with this are Luke 12:48 and James 1:13-16; and Proverbs 25:16 deals directly with the issue of eating sweets (did you know that was even discussed in the Bible? Perhaps God is more concerned with the material details of our lives than many people think.)

4. Do you think that it was more than mere coincidence that Edmund met up with the Queen first when he entered Narnia, while Lucy had first met Mr. Tumnus? Discuss this question.

5. Read over the paragraph on page 42, beginning with "Edmund was already feeling uncomfortable . . ." and ending with "he still wanted to taste that Turkish Delight again more than he wanted anything else." What is it that makes us continue to pursue sinful activities for the sake of a momentary pleasure, even when we know it is wrong and will ultimately have a harmful effect on us that far outweighs any pleasure we could get from it? Romans 7:11-25 is one of the best Biblical passages for explaining this conflict and leading us to the one thing that will enable us to only desire good. How can we help others to discover this and break free from their own sinful bondages?

6. Why do you think Edmund told Lucy "You can't always believe what Fauns say" (page 42)? Often people profess to "know far more about" important issues than we do, therefore claiming the right to dictate to us what we should or should not believe. But they may not really know the Truth any better than we do, and are simply trying to give themselves an excuse to do the wrong thing, and prevent us from doing the right thing. How can we tell when this is the case?

7. Notice how Edmund was annoyed over how he would "have to admit that Lucy had been right" (page 43); and earlier, in talking with the Witch, he belittles his brother and sisters, saying "There's nothing special about *them*" (page 39). Can you make a connection between this kind of stubborn, self-centered pride and one's

willingness to accept the Truth? What do the Scriptures have to say about this question?

8. Read Lucy's final remark on page 43: "what wonderful adventures we shall have now that we're all in it together." In what way is being in a community of other disciples most helpful and uplifting for living a truly fulfilled Christian life? Read Matthew 22:36-40 and Mark 12:28-34, and discuss the implication of the connection between the two Greatest Commandments.

Study Questions for Chapter Five

1. Think about what Edmund did. It was an out-and-out lie, wasn't it? Have you ever met people like Edmund, who know perfectly well that something is real but will falsely deny its existence anyway, out of pure spite? Specifically, have you ever met people who insist that they have not experienced God's Presence or seen signs of His Workings in nature, etc.? And if they *have* experienced such things but just refuse to acknowledge it, would we ever have any way of exposing their own falsehood to them? (Note: many people disparage Christians for "believing in things they cannot prove just because they want to." But could it really be the other way around? Could people *not* believe in God simply because they don't *want* to believe in Him, and not because there isn't proof for His Reality? Think about this, and the answers you would give if someone approached you with this issue of desire vs. reality.)

2. Think about the Professor's statement that "a charge of lying against someone whom you have always found truthful is a very serious thing, a very serious thing indeed" (page 48). Does it make more sense to believe someone who usually tells us the truth, whose story is more inconceivable; or to believe someone who is generally not as truthful, but whose story sounds more plausible? In what way might the argument from authority—believing someone because we believe them to be trustworthy, regardless of how incredible the facts are which they are telling us—be a more reliable argument than it is usually considered in today's society?

3. What do you think of the Professor's logic? Read the "three possibilities" and the conclusion the Professor draws from them on page 48. Is there an instance of something like this in the Christian faith? Where it was either a lie, insanity, or the Truth, and since it couldn't be a lie or insanity, we must accept it as the Truth "[f]or the moment then and unless any further evidence turns up."

4. There was once a great philosopher who said "To be is to be perceived"—in other words, things only exist to the extent that we can see (or touch, or smell, etc.) them. This sounds quite reasonable on the surface, in certain situations, but can you see where the flaws might be in this idea? Go back and read again on page 49, where Peter says "if things are real, they're there all the time" and the Professor replies "Are they?" Now read 2 Corinthians 4:18 and Hebrews 11:1-3. Would you agree with me that these verses indicate that there are realities—very significant realities, in fact—which most of us usually cannot see, but are real nonetheless? (On a side note, that philosopher did believe in such non-perceivable realities himself, in spite of what he said.)

5. Re-read what the Professor has to say on pages 49-50, from "That is the very thing that makes her story so likely to be true" to "I wonder what they *do* teach them at these schools," paying particular attention to his opinion as to the possibility of the existence of different time schemes and different worlds' existence: "Nothing is more probable" (page 50). What do you think? What is the difference between things that simply have not been shown to exist, and things that have been proven to be

impossible to exist? Have you ever noticed that people tend to get these two positions confused?

6. What do you think of the Professor's advice that "[w]e might all try minding our own business" (page 51), and how the subject of the wardrobe was accordingly dropped for some time? When might it be a good idea to spend time doing other things with people without discussing spiritual or moral matters, instead of constantly pressuring them about the same things over and over? Have you ever found it to be the case that someone showed more willingness to listen to the Gospel after you had left the subject alone for a time, to "sink in," until a more favorable opportunity came up to discuss unresolved questions?

Study Questions for Chapter Six

1. Go back and read the beginning of the chapter again, pages 54-55. Did you notice the gradual transformation from the back of the dark wardrobe into the forest, and how none of the others realized what was happening around them from the other signs (the cold, the wetness, etc.) until the light came? How often might this happen to people, that they do not notice the circumstances in their lives that point to the Truth, until the Light shines and reveals all of these circumstances to them as they really are? Read John 1:4-5, 9-14; Matthew 10:26-27; and 2 Corinthians 4:6-7.

2. Notice, on page 55, how quickly Lucy forgave the others and immediately moved on, so that they were all equally companionable once again. Is this very important to do in discipleship, especially with new believers? Read Matthew 5:23-24 and 6:12-15, Luke 17:3-4, and 2 Corinthians 2:4-9. How do these verses demonstrate the importance God places on forgiveness as an absolutely necessary component of the Christian life?

3. Read what Peter says on page 56: "This is going to be exciting enough without pretending." Is living in reality the way God intended it to be better than anything we can make up? Many people spend their lives trying to escape from reality through soap operas and movies and magazines and so forth, simply missing out on the wonderful *real* life God intended them to live. Why would they want to do such a thing?

4. There is an old saying: "No one has a good enough memory to be a successful liar." Notice how easily Edmund gave himself away on

page 56. Do we ever have to be concerned when someone else's lies appear to put us in the wrong, and try to vindicate ourselves? Or can we be certain that they will eventually contradict their own lies and the truth will come out, without our having to do anything at all? Read Numbers 32:23 and 2 Timothy 3:7-9.

5. Think about how Lucy takes the blame for Mr. Tumnus' arrest on page 59, and then go back and read on page 41, how nothing had happened to Mr. Tumnus prior to Edmund's meeting with the Witch. It was Edmund who had given Mr. Tumnus away to the Witch, not Lucy (see page 37). When people do wrong things and go with the wrong crowd, do the effects of their sins often spread beyond themselves to impact the innocent as well? As Christians, can we understand and not blame ourselves when things go wrong, which are simply caused by the presence of sin in the world? As my mother always says, "there is enough sin in the world to account for every trouble, sickness, and misery that occurs." Is it fair that people should have troubles caused by the sins of others? And (this is not the same question) is it *necessary* that they should? Think about this issue, which is often called "the problem of evil."

6. Go back to page 60, and read Peter's point about how "there doesn't seem to be any certainty of getting into this country again when once you've got out of it. I think we'll have to go on." Is this the right approach to take? Is it unwise to turn back once started on an important mission? Read Luke 9:62 again.

7. Re-read Peter and Edmund's discussion at the bottom of page 61 and the top of page 62, to the end of the chapter. What do you think of Edmund's concerns? Do you think that his secret

association with the Witch influenced him in his suspicion of the robin? Also, is he right when he says that they really cannot know which is the right side or who is on the right side (page 62)? Or is Peter right that you can generally trust certain types of people (or birds, in this case) to be on the right side? Do we always have concrete proof of whom we ought to trust and follow or what we ought to do *before* we are required to take action on a critical issue? Can we always demand such proof before taking action? What ought we to do when placed in such circumstances? Read John 16:7-16 and Romans 8:24-28, and see if you can figure it out.

8. Notice that Edmund, in the conversation discussed in the above question, demonstrated actual concern to not alarm his sisters unnecessarily, and raised some rather sensible considerations. But should we think, just because someone can be a nice person sometimes and have some good ideas—practically, morally, or intellectually—that that necessarily means that we can fully trust them?

Study Questions for Chapter Seven

1. Notice how the robin flew away right before the children met Mr. Beaver. Does this ever happen in the Christian life, that one link in God's Plan for us ends before we can see what the next step will be? Read Matthew 6:34.

2. Read the discussion on page 65 from "It wants us to go to it" to "it's no good just standing here." Think back to the final question from the last chapter. What is the connection between thinking, knowing, and risking when trusting in someone?

3. Think about what Peter says on page 65: "We ought to be a match for one beaver if it turns out to be an enemy," and on page 66: "Why, who are you afraid of? . . . There's no one here but ourselves." Is he right? Can we assume that one enemy is just one and that we can deal with it, or could it very well have accomplices lurking out of sight ready to bring us down? Does this work for spiritual enemies and temptations as well? Read Matthew 12:43-45 and 1 Peter 5:8-9. Does God expect us to be cautious and vigilant when it comes to dealing with opponents of His Truth? Read also on page 67, where Edmund and Peter question which side Mr. Beaver is on, and he provides the token. Is it fair to request such a token of trustworthiness?

4. Read over what Mr. Beaver says about the trees on pages 66-67. Can you think of any groups like that in our human world, where most of the members of the group are on the right side and trustworthy; but because some aren't, you can't automatically assume that just because a person belongs to that group that this

necessarily means that they are on the "right side"? Read John 13:10-11, 2 Peter 2:1, and Jude 4-12. How do we know whom to trust, if their declaration of affiliation with a certain group is not sufficient? Read 1 John 4:1-8 and 4:20-5:5.

5. Did it surprise you to read of the children's reactions to the name of Aslan (page 68), even though they didn't know who he was yet? Do people sometimes realize the value of certain spiritual truths and occurrences even when they cannot yet mentally understand or describe the significance of them in their lives? Can we know the Truth and recognize when It is present without necessarily having it explained to us? Try to think of some situations in which this could be the case, for both Christians and non-Christians (or not-yet-Christians).

6. Go back to page 70 and read how "Edmund noticed something else" than the others did. Do people who are occupied with "horrible ideas" see the very same surroundings or circumstances differently than those who think correctly and in accordance with God's Will? And will the plans these two different kinds of people make for dealing with these same circumstances be accordingly different as well? What can we do about such conflicting situations? Is there any way of reconciling the way two people with opposing worldviews view the world? (Read the wording of this last sentence very carefully. Do you notice anything rather unworkable about it?)

7. Read Mrs. Beaver's delighted reception of the children on page 72, where she says, "To think that ever I should live to see this day," as though she had been expecting and hoping for the children to

come for a long time, even though they knew nothing at all about it. If we follow God's leading in our lives, can we end up being the answer to others' hopes and prayers without ever having known that we were going to be? Should we always be prepared to take part in God's plan? Do we—each and every one of us—have a role to play in His Plan? Read Matthew 28:19-20, Romans 10:14-15, and 1 Corinthians 12:4-28.

8. Re-read what Lucy was thinking on page 73, about the Beavers' home in comparison to Mr. Tumnus' cave. What can this tell us, as Christians, about how different kinds of people can all be on the right side, the side of the Lord? Read Mark 9:38-40, Romans 14:1-22, and Galatians 3:28. Discuss the distinction between being different but both on the right side, and being different in the sense that one side is right and the other is clearly wrong, according to Scripture.

Study Questions for Chapter Eight

1. Go back and read page 78 from "can't we—I mean we *must* do something to save him" to "now that Aslan is on the move" and then turn to page 85 and read from "we'll still have to go and look for him" to "That's our only chance now" on page 86. How often, as Christians, do we think that it is our job to save people from evil and danger? Is going into an evil place in an attempt to rescue someone from its influence more likely to result in its influencing *us* wrongly as well, and not saving anyone? Whose job is it to save?

2. See what Edmund says on page 79, "She won't turn him into stone too?" and Mr. Beaver's response. Is it ever possible for evil to fully withstand God's goodness? When confronted with evil powers that are greater than we are, do we ever have to worry about being vanquished and God's plans in us being defeated? Read Romans 8:28-39.

3. Read Mr. Beaver's reply to Lucy's question as to whether Aslan is a man on page 79; and then read Numbers 23:19, Job 40:1-19, Hosea 11:9, Malachi 3:6, John 1:18, and 1 Corinthians 2:16. How often do we expect God to act in accordance with human principles rather than His Own? Would we be less likely to be confused and caught off guard by His actions if we remembered that He is God?

4. Re-read the rhyme about "Adam's flesh and Adam's bone" at the top of page 81 (with both the preceding and following paragraphs), and then read Question One for this chapter again. What is the role we *do* play in God's salvific plan and discipleship? Is it an

important and necessary role? Is there any reason, however, for us to become puffed up about it? Read Matthew 28:18-20, Luke 24:47-49, Romans 12:3-16, and 2 Corinthians 12:7-10.

5. Read Mr. Beaver's remarks about humans and "things that look like humans and aren't" on pages 81-82, up to "keep your eyes on it and feel for your hatchet." Then go back and re-read page 11 and Study Question One for Chapter Two. Are those who deny that humanity is made in the image of God generally dangerous? Could we consider this viewpoint as "ought to be human and isn't" (page 82)? Read Psalm 49:12-20 and 2 Peter 2:10-12. Think of the ingratitude it expresses towards the Creator to not appreciate the unique nature He gave us and act accordingly.

6. On page 85, in the paragraph beginning "Then mark my words" and ending with "something about their eyes," note how Mr. Beaver could tell that Edmund was a traitor just by looking at him, whereas the other children (who were new to Narnia) could not, even though they had known their own brother much longer! Does God give us the ability to discern who is and who is not really a Christian in our midst? Read Malachi 3:18, and compare this verse with Matthew 7:1-6. Discuss whether only those who have "lived long in Narnia" have the ability and the right to make this judgment, whether it could be dangerous or harmful to make such judgments about others without having first developed this ability, and whether it could be equally wrong to fail to use such discernment to preserve the purity of the community of believers. Should Mr. Beaver have immediately brought up and dealt with the matter of Edmund's disregard for the Truth, before he had a

chance to get away and head to betray them? Talk over the pros and cons of both approaches to this kind of situation regarding potential traitors to the faith.

7. Go back and read the paragraph on page 86, where Mrs. Beaver points out that "[h]ow much [Edmund] can tell [the Witch] depends on how much he heard." Is it wise to not discuss our plans for the building up of the Kingdom in front of those who might misinterpret what we say and then go and inform those who are out to hinder God's good purposes and destroy us, who would use their knowledge of our intentions against us? How can we avoid this?

8. Read Mrs. Beaver's practical advice on page 87, and note her insight into what the Witch would do. Is it often the case that believers with supposedly more "minor" roles to play in God's Story actually have deeper discernment in spiritual matters and know better how to use such knowledge practically than the apparently "central" characters, who fulfill prophetic rhymes and become rulers and so forth? Does the amount of glamour attached to one's function in the Kingdom necessarily demonstrate how important this function is in God's eyes? Read Romans 12:3-16 and 1 Corinthians 12:4-27 again, and also Galatians 6:3-10.

Study Questions for Chapter Nine

1. Think about the statement: "there's nothing that spoils the taste of good ordinary food half so much as the memory of bad magic food" on page 88. Do you agree? Read Luke 5:39, John 3:19-21, and James 1:14-17. Also consider, in the light of these verses, why it would be that "the mention of Aslan gave [Edmund] a mysterious and horrible feeling just as it gave the others a mysterious and lovely feeling" (page 88).

2. Do you think that, if Edmund had stayed long enough to hear the "rhyme about *Adam's flesh and Adam's bone* [outlining the pleasant prospects for him if he were to do the right thing] . . . [and] that the White Witch wasn't really human at all but half a Jinn and half a giantess [explaining the rationale for why she had no right to be Queen, and was clearly in the wrong]" (page 89), he would have decided to stay with the others and change to their side? Discuss this question.

3. Go back and read the long paragraph on page 89, beginning from "You mustn't think that even now Edmund was quite so bad . . ." and ending with ". . . deep down inside him he really knew that the White Witch was bad and cruel." Would it help, in witnessing to others, if we remembered that all people generally know the truth about right and wrong, even if they suppress it for selfish reasons, and therefore really can understand and inwardly agree with the principles we stand for as Christians, and are just pretending they don't? Discuss this with the aid of Romans 1:19-20, particularly the final clause: "so that they are without excuse."

4. Why do you think Edmund calls Aslan "awful" when he has never met him or heard anything bad about him? Why do people disparage or condemn those who are good and exercise rightful authority? Is it because they are afraid that those in authority will prevent them from carrying out their own sinful intentions, or can you think of any other reasons? Read Proverbs 29:27, Matthew 20:15, John 7:7, and 1 John 3:12.

5. "The way of transgressors is hard" (Proverbs 13:15). Read over the passage on pages 89-92 describing Edmund's difficult trek through the snow, with his forgetting his coat and all the rest of it. Do you think he would have had quite as hard a time of it if he had been bound on a journey for a good cause? Can wicked intentions make it more difficult to undertake endeavors in the best, most pleasant and practical way?

6. Read on page 92, "it was too late to think of turning back now." When is it too late to turn back from doing wrong?

7. Think about Edmund's experience with the lion, how he was "frightened of a mere statue!" (page 94); and then go and read Proverbs 28:1. Do Christians ever have to be afraid? Are those things that non-Christians are often most afraid of (discuss what these might be) actually nothing at all to fear in reality?

8. Read the paragraph on page 96, about what Edmund did to the statue that was so "silly and childish." Notice particularly how the lion "still looked so terrible, and sad, and noble . . . that Edmund didn't really get any fun out of jeering at it." Can anyone who attempts to ridicule those who are good or who are in misfortune ever really succeed in degrading or embarrassing them? And why

would they want to ridicule them in the first place?—perhaps to make themselves feel greater than they are or to cover up their own feelings of embarrassment over their wrongdoings? Discuss.

9. What did you think when the "stone wolf" on page 97 turned out to be real? Can non-Christians ever guarantee their absolute safety, or can even seemingly foolproof methods for avoiding danger fail us? Read Psalm 146:3 and Proverbs 21:30-31. Who is our only sure Help in trouble?

10. Why do you think Edmund told the White Witch "all he had heard before leaving the Beavers' house" (page 99)? Why do people entrust information, which they know will be used for harmful purposes, to evil rulers? Some people think it is out of a desire to attempt to gain favor and protect oneself. Do you agree? What do you think is going to happen to Edmund next? Is he a "[f]ortunate favorite of the Queen—or else not so fortunate" (page 98)? How can we help people like Edmund to no longer be dependent on wicked "principalities and powers" (Ephesians 6:12) but solely dependent on the One True and Good Ruler over all?

Study Questions for Chapter Ten

1. Notice how calm Mrs. Beaver was about the entire situation at the
    beginning of the chapter. Do Christians ever need to worry about
    even the worst of situations? Read Psalm 91, Proverbs 18:10,
    Matthew 6:27-34, and Philippians 4:6-7.

2. How did you feel when Father Christmas appeared? Some people
    have found fault with C.S. Lewis for using a non-religious
    Christmas symbol as the first sign of the end of the Witch's reign
    in Narnia; what do you think? Does God use human and even
    supposedly "frivolous" things in order to accomplish His
    purposes? Is the arrival of something lighthearted and innocent
    often a sign of God's triumph over the powers of darkness and
    wickedness? Read 1 Corinthians 10:26 and James 1:17, and
    discuss how joy and pleasure are God's gifts to us.

3. Read on page 107, of how the effect of Father Christmas on the
    children was more than "only funny and jolly" and how "Lucy felt
    running through her that deep shiver of gladness which you only
    get if you are being solemn and still." Is there more to real
    happiness (note the adjective "so real" in the description of Father
    Christmas) than mere pleasure and entertainment? Read
    Ecclesiastes 3:1-17, and discuss whether a balance of work and
    play, seriousness and fun, is necessary for a truly joyful Christian
    life.

4. In connection with the last question, discuss the gifts given to the
    children, which were "tools not toys" (page 108), and how much
    they were appreciated as "a very serious kind of present" (page

108). Does God expect us to rejoice as much in the gifts He gives us in order to enable us to do His Work, as in those He gives us just for enjoyment? Read Matthew 25:14-30 or Luke 19:12-27, the Parable of the Talents, and discuss the parable in the light of this question.

5. Consider what Father Christmas says to Lucy on page 109: "But battles are ugly when women fight." Has God given specific roles for women and men to fill individually in this world, and is it to His Glory that we should desire to fulfill our own gender-specific roles? Read and discuss Deuteronomy 22:5 and 1 Corinthians 11:4-15.

6. Read over Father Christmas' farewell of "Merry Christmas! Long live the true King!" (page 109) and talk about the right observance of Christmas before a secular world today.

Study Questions for Chapter Eleven

1. Did it surprise you that Edmund still "expected that the Witch would start being nice to him" (page 111), offered no reaction when she told the Wolf to go to the Beavers' "and kill whatever you find there" (page 113), and felt that the whole experience "seem[ed] like a dream" (page 114)? How often do people unrealistically expect or hope for matters to turn out better than the circumstances and their previous experiences would suggest was reasonable, simply because they have nothing else to hope for?

2. Notice, on page 113, that only the one simple fact that it had begun to snow again prevented the wolves from finding the Beavers and the other children. Was this a mere coincidence or something more? (Read the title to this chapter again.) Does God often use seemingly arbitrary coincidences and everyday occurrences to shape momentous instances of protection and blessing in His children's lives? Authors, in writing stories, very often make something happen which is natural but not necessary (such as it raining or not), without which the goal of the main plot would have failed to turn out as the author (and reader) desired. Does God do the same in writing His story in our lives and the entire universe?

3. They say, "there are no atheists in foxholes." Read where it says on page 114, that "[a]ll the things [Edmund] had said to make himself believe that she was good and kind and that her side was really the right side sounded to him silly now." Is it easier, sometimes, to witness to people when they are going through hard times and realize that this world and its evils do not have the answers they

crave? And do people really try to "make [themselves] believe" that bad things are really good, when they know they are not; and how can we use this knowledge in witnessing to them?

4.   What did you think of the Witch's reaction to the Christmas celebration? Why do you think she cared? Notice how she tried to blame the celebrators and make it sound like their innocent merriment was something bad (as if she cared about anyone doing bad things!), calling it "this gluttony, this waste, this self-indulgence" (page 115). Look up as many verses as you can find (maybe make it a game and see who can find the most) about what the Bible says about hypocrisy, and especially read 1 Timothy 4:1-5. What is it, really, that makes certain behaviors right or wrong, or the same behavior right in one situation and wrong in another, according to Scripture? Read Romans chapter 14, particularly verse 23 (the final verse).

5.   Read how, on page 117, "Edmund for the first time in this story felt sorry for someone besides himself." How does moving outside of oneself and thinking of others impact a Christian life, or anyone's life, for that matter?

6.   How long did it take you to figure out what the thaw meant? Notice how it made Edmund so happy, "though he hardly knew why" (page 118). Talk about how God's miracles and continual triumph over the forces of evil is constantly at work all around us, and how we enjoy it even if we forget to (or are unwilling to) appreciate it, and how we sometimes take them for granted because so many miracles take more time than the instant transformation described in this chapter. (Read the paragraph on

page 119, about "what a relief" the "normal" miraculous change from winter to spring was to Edmund.) Try to see how many miracles you can find in your own life and happening around you in your own everyday experience, which would not usually be described as miracles but really are miracles. What *is* a miracle, exactly (Scripturally, for Christians), anyway?

1. Go back and re-read the paragraph on pages 123-124, beginning
    with "They had been just as surprised . . ." and ending with
    "something had gone wrong, and badly wrong, with the Witch's
    schemes." Do we necessarily have to understand what God is
    doing, or have known previously what He was going to do, in
    order to see His Hand at work in the world and the circumstances
    around us? And do you find it funny that the Witch knew what
    would happen when Aslan came, while the children did not? Do
    the wicked sometimes notice God doing things, and flee from
    them, before the righteous notice Him doing the same things, and
    rejoice over them?

2. Read the line on page 126: "People who have not been in Narnia
    sometimes think that a thing cannot be good and terrible at the
    same time," and then go back to Chapter Eight and re-read the
    discussion about "feel[ing] frightened" (page 80) before Aslan.
    What do you think it would be like to come face to face with
    Jesus? Look up Scripture verses referring to the fear of and the
    awesomeness of God (Exodus 33:18-23, Proverbs 9:10, and
    Jeremiah 32:40 are good places to start) and discuss the two
    equally dangerous extremes of being so afraid of God's just and
    holy Nature that we forget that He is a God of love (see 1 John 4:7-
    8), and that of assuming God to be lenient and tolerant of
    everything and so failing to honor Him properly.

3. Why do you think "Aslan said nothing either to excuse Peter or to
    blame him" (page 128) after Peter confessed that his behavior

towards Edmund may have "helped him to go wrong"? What should our attitude be towards others when they do wrong, if not to get angry at them? What is God's attitude towards us when we sin? Read Exodus 34:7.

4. Read what Aslan says on page 129, about how "[a]ll shall be done . . . But it may be harder than you think," and then how Lucy noticed "that he looked sad as well." We often talk as though nothing bothered God and that His acts on our behalf required no effort or emotional suffering on His part. But is this really true? Think about this. How has God done all for us? And is this "all" harder than we often realize? Read Genesis 6:5-7, Isaiah 53:1-12, John 3:16, 1 Peter 2:21-25, and, if you have time, all the Passion Narratives: Matthew 26:26-27:54, Mark 14:22-15:39, Luke 22:15-24:26, and John 18:8-19:30. You could just pick one of the four to read, but reading all four at once gives a deeper perspective on the whole story.

5. Turn back to pages 129-130, and read the beautiful description of "Cair Paravel of the four thrones, in one of which you must sit as King." What wonders are stored up for God's children to enjoy and reign over? Some marvelous references in Scripture are Psalm 16:11 and all of Psalm 45.

6. Why do you think Peter is to be "High King over all the rest" (page 130), because he is the eldest? Read Genesis 25:25-34; Exodus 13:2, 11-16; and Romans 8:17, 29. What is the Biblical prerogative and responsibility of the firstborn, and what does this typify or point to spiritually?

7. What do you think the significance was in Aslan's reminding Peter to clean his sword (pages 132-133)? Was it a reminder that God's children may have to be involved in dangerous and even disturbing events such as war, but must do so differently and from purer motives than the rest of the world? Sometimes non-Christians (and even some Christians) talk as though Christian love and behavior were inconsistent with military acts, or any acts of vigilance, justice, and valor. Read Matthew 10:34-39 and 26:52-56, noting the context of both statements; and then read how Peter felt about the whole experience on pages 131-132, and how Aslan said "Let the Prince win his spurs" (page 130). Are there parallels between being a Christian and being a soldier? Read Joshua 1:1-9 and 5:13-6:7, and 2 Timothy 2:3-4 and 4:7.

Study Questions for Chapter Thirteen

1. Read what the Witch says about the prophecy on pages 134-135: "How if only three were filled . . ." and discuss. Are there certain conditions that must be humanly/naturally fulfilled in order for God's prophecies to come to pass? And if so, how then does God ensure that His promises always *will* come to pass? Read Esther 4:7-14.

2. On page 138, note that "it was part of [the Witch's] magic that she could make things look like what they aren't." Is this a common trick of the evil one to tempt and deceive? Look up 2 Corinthians 11:13-15, and see what it has to say about this.

3. Did you notice the passage on page 139 where it was specifically mentioned that "[t]here is no need to tell you (and no one ever heard)" what Aslan and Edmund were discussing, and note how this unheard discussion led to a complete change in Edmund's thinking? Are there parts of conversion which are simply between the specific person and God; and if so, what should we leave to Him and what is our role? Read on further down the page to see what the rest of the children did. What do you think?

4. What did you think when Peter told Lucy on page 140, about the two leopards, "It'll be all right . . . He wouldn't send them if it weren't"? How often do we fear that something bad will happen to us even when we are following God's instructions, as though He didn't know and couldn't protect us from any dangers in the path? Why is it wrong to feel this way, and why was what Peter said so commendable, according to Scripture?

5. On page 141, note how "Edmund had got past thinking about himself . . . He just went on looking at Aslan. It didn't seem to matter what the Witch said." Do we ever have to be humiliated by what the world says about us (possibly dredging up things in our past that we have done wrong), once we are Christians and have our eyes on God? Can anyone really shame us before Him? And if they cannot shame us before Him, who *could* they shame us before? Read Romans 8:30-34 and discuss.

6. Go back and re-read the discussion about the "Deep Magic" (pages 141-142) very carefully, beginning with "You have a traitor there, Aslan . . ." and ending with "nobody ever made that suggestion to him again." Especially notice Aslan's reaction to Susan's suggestion that he "[w]ork against the Emperor's Magic" (page 142). Is it the case, that God has set up the world in such a way that evil consequences (which are of course part of the forces of evil) *must* come in response to evil decisions we humans make and sinful acts we commit? Read Genesis 2:17, Proverbs 16:4, Ezekiel 18:20-32, and Galatians 6:7-8. And is this the only right way, consistent with God's Perfect Holiness, in which He *could* have set the world up? Could He ever work against His Own principles in any case? Read Exodus 3:14, Matthew 26:36-56, Mark 14:32-49, Luke 22:40-53, John 6:37-40 and 18:11, and 2 Timothy 2:13, particularly the Garden of Gethsemane accounts. Why could Aslan never work against the Emperor-beyond-the-Sea? Also consider, in the light of these verses, the question that agnostic and atheistic mockers often ask Christians: "Could God make a stone so big He couldn't lift it Himself?" and this quote from the eighteenth-

century German philosopher Leibniz: "this is the best of all possible worlds." Is he right?

7. Read over again what the Witch says right before Mr. Beaver's interjected remark about "you were the Emperor's hangman" (what does that mean, anyway?) on pages 141-142, and on down to " . . . unless I have blood as the Law says all Narnia will be overturned and perish in fire and water." What is this "Law" she is talking about? Can it be possible for an instrument of God's work to "go to the bad" by focusing attention only on itself and gaining power for itself, instead of on performing its own proper function in God's plan? Could this happen with ideologies as well as with individual people? Discuss. And can even bad things sometimes play a role (without intending to) in God's plan, by Him turning them around and working with them to bring good out of evil? Read Genesis 45:5-8 and 50:20, Proverbs 16:4 again, and Romans 7:7-25.

8. The final sentence of this chapter is one of my favorite lines in *The Lion, the Witch, and the Wardrobe*, when the Witch "fairly ran for her life" (page 144). Does it delight you, too, and give you a feeling of sharing in God's Victory, whenever we are enabled to witness His Power overcoming all that dares to come against Him? Read Romans 8:31-37. Is it not truly amazing, that the most powerful of worldly forces are as nothing before the very smallest demonstration of God's Power or even just His mere Presence? Read Psalms 18:13-15 and 68:2, Hosea 11:10, and 2 Thessalonians 2:8.

1. On page 146, Aslan says "I can give you no promise" of being at the battle. Why does he say this? When, if ever, does God leave us to carry out certain functions in this world without His direct intervention? The following verses may be helpful in discussing this question: Psalm 22, Luke 22:53, and especially John 16:7-16.

2. Notice how miserable Aslan was in the beginning of this chapter. Does God ever suffer from grief like this? Read Matthew 26:37-38, Luke 22:44, and John 11:33-38.

3. Why does Aslan tell the girls to leave him "to go on alone" on page 149? What is it that only God can do and we must leave entirely to Him, having no influence or merit in the matter? See Ephesians 2:5-9.

4. Why didn't Aslan do anything to the evil crowd taunting him, even though he could have easily destroyed them all? Why were they all still afraid of him, in that case?

5. Go back and read on page 151, where it says "I won't describe [the other evil creatures] because if I did the grown-ups would probably not let you read this book." How much do we need to know about evil in order to confront it, and when is it best that Christians remain in entire ignorance regarding it? Read Ephesians 5:11-12 and 1 Thessalonians 5:22.

6. The mockery of the Witch's followers didn't demean Aslan at all (see page 153). Often people turn away from doing things God's way because they have been told it will lead to their being

humiliated. Why are we afraid of being humiliated? What can or can't really humiliate and degrade us?

7. Discuss the obvious parallelism between this chapter and the Biblical account of the Atonement. How can a literary work, or other things in the world (such as the self-sacrifice of soldiers in war), reflect or convey the message to us of what God has done?

1. Notice how the girls' grief over Aslan's death was greater than their fear of what might happen to them. And on page 158, it suggests that after experiencing such sorrow and realizing the full extent of its horror, "[y]ou feel as if nothing was ever going to happen again." In what way does Christ's suffering of the worst misery ever experienced free us from further concern over our own worldly trials?

2. Why did Susan want to chase the mice away? How often do we assume the worst of those who are really trying to help?

3. What does the cracking of the Stone Table, when Aslan rises, represent? Read Exodus 32:15-19 and 34:1, and Romans 8:2.

4. Why did Susan worry (as the disciples did at first about Christ) that Aslan was a ghost? What is the difference between the Christian belief in the resurrection of the body and purely spiritual notions of an otherworldly existence after death? A good passage to consult here is 1 Corinthians 15:35-58.

5. How is it that the "Deeper Magic from Before the Dawn of Time," as Aslan explains it to the girls on page 163, can overcome the Deep Magic without "working against" it, as Aslan said was impossible back on page 142? Read Matthew 5:17-18 and Romans 10:4, and discuss. How does Christ by fulfilling the Law abolish the claims of the Law? What does this mean, and in what way are we still "under the law to Christ" (1 Corinthians 9:21)?

6. Think about how the very first thing the girls and Aslan do after he is risen is to romp and have fun. What is it that makes being a

Christian so much fun? Why is rejoicing such an intrinsic part of God's plan for His Creation?

7. Why does Aslan roar? What does it indicate that he is going to do, as "his face became so terrible that they did not dare to look at it" (page 164), even though they were so happy?

8. Why did the girls have to ride on Aslan? When do we have to submit ourselves to God's carrying in order to get to where He wants us to go?

1. What does the slight lapse of time before the stone lion returns fully to life again signify?

2. Why do you think Aslan's breathing on the statues is what restores them to life? Could it be comparable to anything specific in Christian experience? You might want to look up the following verses for clues: Ezekiel 37:1-14, John 3:5-8 and 20:21-22, and Acts 2:1-4.*

3. What did you think of Aslan's reply to Susan's concern about the giant on page 169? Did it surprise you? Do you think he may have known what Susan really meant? And do you think that God may find our concerns about how He is taking care of certain matters in our own lives funny? In what way?

4. Why did Aslan utilize the help of Giant Rumblebuffin and the other lion? Did he really need their help? Why does God involve us in His mission for the Gospel? Could His plans for the full redemption of the world work out without His people helping other people, with the work of salvation being solely between Him and each individual separately? Discuss the importance of Christian communion.

5. Why did Aslan give the other lion more work as a way of tempering his conceit? Why was the other lion so delighted about getting to work with Aslan? Talk about the humbling responsibility

---

*By the way, in the Greek language, the translations for "breath," "spirit," and "wind" are all the same word. What do you think about this connection?

of being involved in God's work—can you think of any real-life examples?

6. However, despite the involvement of the other creatures, it is Aslan alone who kills the Witch. What does this mean about God's Sovereignty?

Study Questions for Chapter Seventeen

1. How has Peter shown himself to be a true Christian leader? Think about how, at the end of the last chapter, on page 176, he was the one fighting the White Witch herself until Aslan arrived. What is it that entitles someone to the position of a leader? Is it that the person possesses better qualities for leadership than another, or simply that he has been the one to take on the position of leadership and fulfill its demands as necessary in the situation? Does God call everybody to be a leader? And when called, should one's apparent lack of abilities hold him back from following the call? Read Exodus 3:11-4:18, Isaiah 6:1-8, Jeremiah 1:4-10, and 1 Corinthians 12:4-28 (again).

2. Why did Lucy have to wait and go help others before knowing how the cordial would restore Edmund? How might this have increased her unselfishness of character and faith in Aslan? Do we have a right to expect God to reassure us fully as to the state of our own concerns before we must go and help others with theirs?

3. Think of what Aslan says on page 179: "Must *more* people die for Edmund?" What does this say about the significance of Christ's one-time redemption? There is an interesting Scriptural connection here to the story of Moses and the rock in Numbers 20:2-12. What does this say about the serious consequences of downplaying the essential nature of Christ's sacrifice for us when we try to solve the world's problems ourselves?

4. Edmund was cured of more than his wounds. What had really happened to him, between the battle, Aslan's sacrifice, and the

cordial? (which was, of course, the gift of Aslan. You might want to go back to Chapter Ten, and re-read the part about Father Christmas.) And why was it that, even though Aslan had paid the price for him, Edmund still had to fight in the battle and suffer so terribly in his cause? What does this mean for us, as Christian "martyrs" (which means "witnesses" in Greek), of today?

5. Which do you agree with, Susan or Lucy, in their discussion on pages 180-181, as to whether or not Edmund should be told "what Aslan did for him?" Do you think Edmund ever did know? Do you think he already knew? If so, how?

6. What does it mean to be "Once a king or queen in Narnia, always a king or queen" (page 182)? How must such a privilege be "borne well"?

7. What does it mean, in Mr. Beaver's famous phrase on page 182, that Aslan is "wild, you know. Not like a *tame* lion." Discuss what it would mean for God to be "tame," and what it means for us since He is not.

8. Why do you think the Kings and Queens decided to go on past the lamp-post, to discover what it meant? Were they wise to do so? Discuss whether that was what Aslan would have wanted them to do.

9. The Professor's final speech, on pages 188-189, starting with "Yes, of course you'll get back to Narnia again someday" and ending with "Bless me, what *do* they teach them at these schools?" is probably my favorite passage to quote from all of C.S. Lewis' writings. Why does he caution the children to not "talk too much about it even among yourselves"? Are there mysteries of God that

are better just experienced when He decides to reveal them to us, and not analyzed too much on our own? What other concerns should we be occupying our minds with while on earth as Christians? And have you ever had an experience such as the Professor mentions, when you just can't help knowing that someone else is a Christian, even if neither one of you has mentioned it yet? What is it that draws us all together in the knowledge of Christ?

Overall Study Questions for *The Lion, the Witch, and the Wardrobe*

1. Can you summarize, in your own words, what the core Christian message of *The Lion, the Witch, and the Wardrobe* is?

2. What are the three most important things you can take away from this book for your own Christian walk and life?

3. How would you respond if someone asked you a question about the connection between Christianity and *The Lion, the Witch, and the Wardrobe*? Would you use examples from the book to answer general questions about or challenges against Christianity? Which ones?

www.ingramcontent.com/pod-product-compliance
Lightning Source LLC
Chambersburg PA
CBHW021117020426
42331CB00004B/525